Robby the C-130 Goes To Germany

Written by Beth Mahoney
Illustrated by Zachary Porter

**Military Children Serve Too and
We are so Proud of You!**

This book is provided by the 153d Airlift
Wing, Wyoming Air National Guard,
Airman and Family Readiness Program
in celebration of the
Month of the Military Child
April 2011

Dedicated to Madelyn,
the best mother-in-law a military wife
could ever ask for.

www.RobbyTheC130.com

Robby is packing his suitcase today. He has to go away for a while. He is going to a country called Germany (sounds like Jur-muh-nee). Robby's soldier friends need him again and it is his job to go where the military needs him. He will be transporting supplies and vehicles around Europe.

Robby's little sister, Rachel, does not want Robby to go away again. She is sad. She does not understand where Germany is, so Robby shows her some pictures of Germany.

Robby tells Rachel that Germany is a country in Central Europe (sounds like yoor-up). Germany has all four of the seasons: Summer, Spring, Fall, and Winter. It does not get very hot in the summer, but it can get very cold in the Winter.

Robby tells her that there is a lot to do in Germany. There are beautiful castles, parks and gardens. Germany also holds fun and colorful festivals. Rachel thinks that is neat and dances around like a Princess in a castle.

Robby shows Rachel a picture of where he is flying to on a map. He tells her it will take him an entire day to get to Germany from the United States. Rachel spins the hands on a clock to show how long one day is.

Robby's little brother, Alex, overhears them talking about Germany and he asks if they play any cool sports like Soccer. Robby tells Alex that Soccer had been the most popular game in West Germany. In 1954, 1974, and 1990 West Germany won the world cup. Alex is amazed. Soccer is his favorite sport!

Robby also tells Alex that Germany makes some really cool cars too, like the Porsche, the Audi, the Volkswagen, and their mom's favorite, the BMW. Alex thinks Germany might be a pretty cool country to visit.

Rachel wants to know if Robby will write to her. Robby tells her that he will send postcards with pictures of Germany so that she can collect them in her travel diary. Rachel is so excited that she begins to draw the first page in her book of Germany.

Robby says that he will even go hiking in the forests of Northern Hesse where there are sparkling lakes and amazing views of the valley. He says he will send pictures of the fields of flowers so Rachel can put those in her book too.

Alex tells Robby that he doesn't want pictures, he would rather have a souvenir. A souvenir is a small gift that reminds you of the places you hav visited. Robby tells Alex he will bring back something for everyone.

Alex is curious if they speak English in Germany. Robby tells him that where he is going there are a lot of American soldiers and their families, so they speak English, but outside of the base, the Germans speak German. Alex wants to know if Robby has learned any German words. Robby tells him a few German words and what they mean.

Alex wants to know if Germans dress differently from Americans. Robby tells him that there really is not much of a difference. Germans like to wear jeans and t-shirts or dresses just like Americans, but most Germans do not like the big basketball sneakers and baggy clothes that American teenagers tend to wear.

Rachel asks Robby how long he will be in Germany. Robby tells her he is going over to a base called Ramstein Air Force Base for a few months. The Military calls it a "Temporary Duty" or a "TDY". That Means he is Not staying over there to live, but just to visit until his work is done.

Ramstein Air Force Base is located near the town of Ramstein, in the rural district of Kaiserslautern (sounds like Kahy-zerz-lou-tern), Germany. It is the headquarters for the United States Air Forces in Europe.

Rachel is sad again. This time she is more sad that she will not be going with Robby. She wants to see Germany too! It sounds like such a great place and very beautiful. Maybe someday when she grows into her new propellers she will be big enough to fly to Germany and visit. Until then, she can't wait to get the pictures from Robby to add to her book.

THE END

MY Germany
Picture Diary

Rachel's travel diary holds lots of pictures throughout the world. Create your own picture diary to share with your family and friends! You can paste your own pictures or draw them.

My Name Is:

_____

Paste or draw a picture of Germany

DATE: _____ __   PLACE: _____

ABOUT THIS PICTURE:

_____

_____

_____

Paste or draw a picture of Germany

DATE: _____ __   PLACE: _____

ABOUT THIS PICTURE:

_____

_____

_____

Paste or draw a picture of Germany

DATE: _____ ___   PLACE: _____

ABOUT THIS PICTURE:

_____

_____

_____

Paste or draw a picture of Germany

DATE: _____ ___   PLACE: _____

ABOUT THIS PICTURE:

_____

_____

_____

- **Destination Germany**
  http://viewer.zmags.com/publication/2c241822#/2c241822/20

- **Ramstein AFB**
  http://www.ramstein.af.mil/

- **Germany Tourism**
  http://www.germany-tourism.de/

- **Amiexpat**
  http://www.amiexpat.com

And to all our military friends who have lived
or traveled to Germany and provided some insight.

Military Children's Resources

Military Child Education Coalition (MCEC)

http://www.militarychild.org/

MCEC is a 501(c)(3) non-profit, world-wide organization that identifies the challenges that face the highly mobile military child, increases awareness of these challenges in military and educational communities, and initiates and implements programs to meet the challenges.

Operation: Military Kids (OMK)

http://www.operationmilitarykids.org/public/home.aspx

The U.S. Army's collaborative effort with 4H and America's communities to support the children and youth of National Guard and Army Reserve Soldiers impacted by the Global War on Terrorism.

Kids of Americas Heroes

http://www.koahprogram.com

Non-profit organization for military children whose parent(s) are deployed, on a remote, or temporary duty assignment. Koah provides activities and entertainment for after school programs.

Robby the C-130

http://www.robbythec130.com

The official website of Robby the C-130 and friends. Visit Robby online to see pictures, videos, and download activities.

The Military Impacted Schools Association (MISA)

http://www.militaryimpactedschoolsassociation.org/

A national organization representing school districts that serve high concentrations of military children. The organization works to provide a continuum of quality education through funding, legislation, partnerships and programs for military families on the move. MISA also offers training sessions for principals on the use of the DoD's "Tools for Schools" in their districts.

National Military Family Association (NMFA)

http://www.nmfa.org/

"The Voice for Military Families," is dedicated to providing information to and representing the interests of family members of the uniformed services. Providing information on deployment, education, family life and health care, and resources.

About the Author

Beth Mahoney is a military brat turned military wife and proud mother of three. Aside from writing the Robby the C-130 Series (*www.robbythec130.com*), Mrs. Mahoney is President of Kids of Americas Heroes (*www.koahprogram.com*), a non-profit organization for military children, where she works with local elementary schools and military networks to provide more support and resources for military families. Mrs. Mahoney attended Hawaii Pacific University. In 2009 she become Volunteer of the Quarter for Little Rock AFB, and is an active member of the Air Force Association, National Military Family Association, and the AFSA.

For interviews, book signing events, or school activities please contact Beth Mahoney at bmahoney@robbythec130.com or visit www.robbythec130.com

Collect the Robby the C-130 Series
and look for more Robby the C-130
books coming soon!

Kids of Americas Heroes

6879791R0

Made in the USA
Lexington, KY
29 September 2010